Dr K M A Ahamed Zubair

…l) and its Intricate Narrative Layers

Dr K M A Ahamed Zubair

Adore Me (Arabic Novel) and its Intricate Narrative Layers

Novelist Sana Sha'lan's Overflow of Love's Language

Noor Publishing

Imprint

Any brand names and product names mentioned in this book are subject to trademark, brand or patent protection and are trademarks or registered trademarks of their respective holders. The use of brand names, product names, common names, trade names, product descriptions etc. even without a particular marking in this work is in no way to be construed to mean that such names may be regarded as unrestricted in respect of trademark and brand protection legislation and could thus be used by anyone.

Cover image: www.ingimage.com

Publisher:
Noor Publishing
is a trademark of
Dodo Books Indian Ocean Ltd. and OmniScriptum S.R.L publishing group

120 High Road, East Finchley, London, N2 9ED, United Kingdom
Str. Armeneasca 28/1, office 1, Chisinau MD-2012, Republic of Moldova, Europe
Printed at: see last page
ISBN: 978-620-7-47908-5

Adore Me (Arabic Novel) and its Intricate Narrative Layers

Novelist Sana Sha'lan's Overflow of Love's Language

Dr.K.M.A.Ahamed Zubair

Associate Professor of Arabic, The New College, Chennai 600 014, India

اللغة العربية تحمل كلمة الله، وروح محمد ﷺ، وسر الإسلام،

This work has been dedicated to the Indian Islamic
Missionaries (1500-1800)

Preface

In the exploration of literature, there exists a realm where words transcend mere expression; they become conduits for unraveling the tapestry of human existence. 'Adore Me' stands as an epitome of such an enigmatic realm, where the interplay of love, identity, and the fusion of consciousness with the physical form unfolds in captivating complexity.

This research is an odyssey into the heart of 'Adore Me,' a literary work that defies conventions and beckons readers into a world teeming with symbolism, social commentary, and profound philosophical introspection. Through meticulous analysis and careful examination, this study embarks on a journey to decipher the layers of meaning woven intricately into the text.

Within these pages lies an endeavor to unravel the mysteries concealed within the narrative's depths, to illuminate the brilliance of the author's craft, and to unearth the truths and inquiries that resonate beyond the confines of its pages. It is an expedition into the realms of love's language, where every word carries weight, every character embodies a dimension, and every interaction beckons contemplation.

This preface serves as an invitation to traverse the landscapes of 'Adore Me,' to embrace the complexities it presents, and to embark upon a scholarly exploration that seeks not only to analyze but to embrace the essence of a work that pulsates with the vitality of love as the bedrock of existence.

Join in this expedition as we navigate through the realms of literature and uncover the myriad facets of 'Adore Me,' a literary gem that stands as a testament to the enduring power of storytelling and the profundity of the human experience.

Dr K M A Ahamed Zubair

Contents

Adore Me: Overflow of Love's Language

Introduction

The analysis of 'Adore Me' delves into the intricacies of a literary work that intricately weaves together themes of love, identity, and the fusion of human consciousness with the physical form. This research aims to dissect the text's multifaceted narrative and explore the layers of symbolism and social commentary embedded within.

Purpose

The primary objective of this research is to unravel the narrative techniques, thematic underpinnings, and the interplay of characters in 'Adore Me.' By dissecting the author's construction of a world where love transcends dimensions, this study aims to elucidate the philosophical depth and social critiques hidden within the text.

Methodology

Utilizing a close textual analysis approach, this research delves into the text's nuances, examining character development, narrative structure, and thematic elements. Additionally, comparative analysis with similar literary works by other authors like Tahar Wattar and Halima Zine El Abidine provides a broader context for understanding the unique aspects of 'Adore Me.'

Findings

The analysis uncovers a complex portrayal of a character, Basil Al-Mahri, whose consciousness merges with a female body, challenging conventional notions of identity and gender. The exploration of this amalgamation of mind and physical form raises questions about adaptation, identity acceptance, and societal norms.

Originality of Research

This research contributes to literary scholarship by offering an in-depth exploration of 'Adore Me,' elucidating its unique narrative structure, thematic depth, and social commentary. The comparative analysis with other literary works enriches the understanding of this text's originality and distinctiveness.

Content of the Article

The article's content traverses various dimensions present in 'Adore Me,' including the portrayal of characters, the fusion of human consciousness with machine-like existence, and the exploration of love as a foundational element of existence. Additionally, it navigates through the intricate interplay of pronouns, exchanges between characters, and the convergence of timelines, all within the realm of boundless love and existential secrets.

In conclusion, 'Adore Me' emerges as a compelling literary work that deftly intertwines elements of love, identity, and societal commentary. Through a detailed analysis, this research illuminates the text's depth and originality, underscoring its contribution to contemporary literary discourse and its powerful portrayal of the human condition.

'Adore Me': Overflow of Love's Language
An Analytical Study

Since the rise of contemporary critical school concepts, the title has garnered the interest of researchers and critics. It became a fundamental starting point for entering the text when the title extends its ramifications within the content. Many authors may place it arbitrarily or for commercial purposes, neglecting this dimension that turns it into a key or a concentrated sign summarizing the text, thereby referring one to the other. If it achieves this kind of indication and stimulation from the beginning, casting its shadow throughout the text, there's no point in considering whether the writer placed it before composing the text or after in the revision stage, or whether it emerged at the moment of writing.

Hence, it can be said that choosing the present verb in 'Adore Me' does not indicate a pure present or a pure future; rather, it embodies a state of permanence and continuity, besides the mystical charge that love holds, making it the secret of existence.

If she said, 'I adore myself or my essence,' that would be linguistically correct, except this form implants a sense of detachment between the active verb and the object, widening the distance between the two in articulation and feeling. But when the writer chose the concealed and attached first-person pronoun, the distance significantly shrinks, and the protective noon only represents a simple barrier, allowing the self to merge with the self, rendering it impossible to become a single word or a single embodiment.

The text seems to describe a character, Basal Al-Mahri, who, after losing his body in a loyal war for the state, remains with a male mind. Doctors, assisted by galactic intelligence, consider performing a unique surgery for him to inhabit a female body temporarily while waiting to find a male body.

This imaginative image is similar to the approach used by Algerian writer Tahar Wattar in his novel "Love and Death in El Harrazi Time," where he portrays a character, Brahma, dividing his body into a man and a woman. Similarly, Moroccan writer Halima Zine El Abidine presents a comparable scenario in her novel "It Was Not a Desert," discussing the creation of a being with dual aspects.

However, in Sanaa Sha'lan's case, the woman

chosen to host the mind of this man is not like other women. She's described as a respected national leader in the forbidden and oppositional Life Party. She, a renowned writer, suffers imprisonment and torture, while Basal Al-Mahri was a commissioned person fighting rebels and activists for the intelligence state. He lives with a mechanical mind, devoid of feelings of humanity and love, while the woman embodies compassion and affection, elements he lacks.

The passage depicts a character whose brain merges with a body to such an extent that distinguishing between genders becomes nearly impossible. This literary technique reflects the era where humans lean towards machine-like existence, bound by the strictness of materialistic and electronic intellect, leading to a spiritual emptiness.

The author's preference for flying on the wings of imagination towards the fourth millennium suggests that this reckless and arrogant person might have realized the necessity of uniting mind and heart, symbolized by "Khaled," the hopeful figure representing pure humanity, deserving of adoration and eternal bliss.

While this depiction may seem unfamiliar and strange, it also creates tension and perplexing questions, prompting the reader to anticipate what unfolds. Will there be resentment toward the unfamiliar body attached, even though it's innocent or perhaps weaker, or more beautiful? Or "is it due to its tenderness and compassion towards the protagonist's growing childhood resentment for losing their body"?

The man faces an unprecedented operation, uncertain of its success, within the body of a slender woman ravaged by torture. This situation paints a vivid picture of loss in the soul, with the surroundings symbolizing a profound emptiness.

The text portrays a scenario where a strong-brained individual, Basil Al-Mahri, is merged with a female body, raising questions about whether his brain will adapt to the strong, muscular body it once inhabited. Will doctors eventually find a male body for him in the near future, or is this a doubtful prospect? Complicating matters further, the foreign body gradually swells, surprising him with the presence of a moving fetus.

The unfolding events intensify tension, presented not all at once but in gradual sequences, prompting anticipation and a need for patience. The directional arrows in the following diagram indicate the flow of conversation between characters, with a single -headed arrow denoting the narrator's speech to the recipient and the double-headed arrow symbolizing their mutual exchange.

The novel creates a complex world where body meets mind and man merges with machine. The increasing tension accompanies every new development, raising the crucial question: will this unconventional connection between mind and body succeed? Will Basil regain his male body, or will he remain trapped in the growing female body, harboring a moving fetus within, stirred by tension and anxiety?

The novel appears rich in captivating tensions and intriguing questions, focusing on the intersection of human and technological facets vividly depicted through this world crafted by the author.

The function of (Bassam, Shams, Khaled, and Ward) opens up a wide narrative horizon that ripples across several levels:

1. The author begins the text in a manner that doesn't explicitly assign a gender to the general narrative by using the absent pronoun speaker: "Only those with loving hearts perceive the reality of existence beyond the four dimensions governing this vast universe. I am not against the dimensions of length, width, height, and time... But I, with absolute

certainty, know that love is the fifth dimension that shapes our existence." The author finds no suitable place for sick humans outside the hospital, making the hospital the only space where the narrative fabric aligns. Therefore, Shams appears parentless because she belongs to everyone through the love she possesses. The author challenges the legitimacy of conventional marital relationships, portraying them as insufficient to elevate individuals beyond the animalistic sexual practice to higher, nobler realms.

2. The novel comprises eight chapters, each adorned with dimensions beyond length, such as the extension of one's body, concepts of time, and additional relative theories beyond height and width. However, the fifth dimension, love, pulsates through all chapters, altering the realities of things and the laws of nature. The

subsequent three chapters express the release of hidden love energy, progressing with a linguistic flow that entices rather than hinders the narrative progression.

3. A binary relationship emerges between Bassam, represented by the brain, and the fetus, positioning the latter as the addressed entity. Additionally, a second binary relationship forms between Shams and the fetus, and a third between Shams and Khaled.

In the first instance, the dialogue takes the form of a plea, addressing the fetus, which occasionally moves silently, evoking constant concern due to its prolonged stay in the womb. In the second scenario, the addressed becomes a little girl because, to Bassam, Ward is a child, and to her mother, she remains a child.

"Your name will be Ward, a name chosen for you by Khaled. From now on, I can almost smell your rosy scent. You pulse within my motherly heart, my little rose. It's a collection of the word 'rose,' a beautiful plant with a fragrant scent (...). The rose is also the name of an extinct animal from a time before the fourth millennium. It's also called the lion, a predatory, wild, powerful, and noble creature that lives with pride, dies with pride, refuses submission, and treasures its strength. Hence, we named you Ward, dedicated to beauty, strength, and our love" .

In the third scenario, the interaction happens through messages written by Khaled and the stories/morals he narrates.

This interplay of pronouns and exchanges between the narrator and the narrated, as well as the intertwining of timelines, imbues the text with diversity, providing the recipient with the chance to navigate through different and intriguing atmospheres, all converging in an infinite space of boundless love, which is the secret of existence. Simultaneously, it aspires to a time beyond the present bleak era we live in.

Bassam continues flipping through her notes until reaching the blank pages. Once saturated with affection and tenderness, and filled with eternal love, she beseeches the child, saying, "What do you think about being born on the moon, Ward? This is your mother's desire. Tomorrow, we will travel there; you have many relatives in that place. Your mother doesn't know you're a boy; she thinks you're a girl, but your father will know you're a man. Exceptional like him, do you love your father, Ward? You must do so. I love him very much, and I love your mother even more. Let me tell you a secret: I am passionately in love with your mother, deeply in love with myself."

This novel perceives love as the foundation of existence, emphasizing that in its absence, humans become victims of a repugnant automatic mechanism, swimming in a spiritual void and a quagmire of moral degradation. The novel, in this sense, critiques a political and social reality through allusion rather than direct statement. Successful literature often plays the game of alternation and concealment by its nature.

Moreover, the word)حب‎("love," comprising

only two letters, takes on an infinite dimension due to the philosophy and existential depth infused by the author. It intertwines the real with the imaginary, blends literary imagery with Sufi indications, and integrates short poetic pieces expressing longing, prayers, emotions, and fervency. All of this is made possible by Sanaa's expressive energy and a powerful language that stretches across extensive mental landscapes, presenting us with a single idea donned in a new literary garb from paragraph to paragraph. Those who wish to speak solely about the novel's language will find it worthy of a meticulous independent study, a task beyond this initial impression.

A Reading in the novel 'A'ashoquni' by the author Dr. Sanaa Al-Shaalan:

In the scope of criticism, precisely through acknowledging that it is language alone, the image is a more accurate 'behind-the-language' language. It becomes paradoxically antithetical, yet authentically, objectively, historically, existentially, collectively, and liberally. The language chosen by the critic to speak is not a gift from heaven but one among many languages presented by its position in time. It is objectively the final stage of the historical evolution of knowledge, ideas, and intellectual ramifications; it is a necessity. On the other hand, every critic chooses this necessary language according to a certain existential pattern, as a means of a functional intellectual practice unique to themselves, thus embedding in this process their deepest preferences, resistance pleasures, forms of obsession. In this way, the critical work contains within itself a dialogue between two historical positions and two selves: the position of the author and their self, and the position of the critic and their self. However, this dialogue reveals a complete bias towards the present; criticism is not a homage leading to the truth of the past or the truth of the other present. Instead, it's an arrangement of that clear perception in our time.

'A'ashoquni': a novel of love and a magical love affair. 'I love, therefore I exist' and scientific imagination simultaneously. Its events are set temporally in the fourth millennium, in a place where science is still urging forward to grasp it for settlement. The novelist, Sanaa Al-Shaalan, precedes them with her imagination by erasing the path of the predictable, allowing the transformed lover to live on one of his planets after being freed from six cosmic wars that uprooted humanity from the earth we live on. It summoned it as a fifth cosmic dimension, as known by the dimension of love, after humanity tired of the dominance of hatred and wars that crushed its dreams and hopes, leaving destruction and injustice behind.

The novel 'A'ashoquni' is a problematic novel from its very first title, the cornerstone of the narrative work and its associative relationship with the narrative text. This ensnared many readers and critics in the intended deception by the novelist, stirring the reader's imagination and immersing them in the labyrinth of meaning, insisting on continuing their delightful maze. They start searching for the profitability of the verb 'A'ashoquni,' hinging on pronunciation and hearing, stimulating the question in the recipient: is 'A'ashoquni' referring to the hidden narrator 'the author' or to 'I,' the protagonist of the novel? It's a maze that stimulates pleasure and provokes the imagination in the quest for the implications of 'A'ashoquni.' Hence, the disappointment arises, the horizon of the reader's anticipation, and this difference between the author's writing and the reader's anticipation is called the aesthetic distance according to 'Yaos,' which defines it as the distance between the appearance of the literary trace itself and the recipient's anticipation from the very first entry, the title. The nature of reading and the mechanism of interpretation that seek understanding according to the reader's perceptions always entail the beginning of interpretation, i.e., the formulation of meaning also integrates perception.

The critical reading of any literary work seeks to reveal its aesthetic dimensions, relying on the critic-reader's balance and their socio-cultural and critical knowledge to break the monopoly of meaning. The reader has become a collaborator in the imaginative creation of the text through their knowledge and 'aesthetic integrity.' So, we face a problematic title built on allegory that arouses the reader's curiosity in tracing it to reach the latent linguistic meaning because it's an associative suggestive title. We need to dissect it through reading the novel. This is an exceptionally smart game imposed by the novelist 'the title,' compelling us to enter the inner openings of the novel, revealing that it's a science fiction novel but simultaneously a romantic love story of the highest order. It's written in a poetic language with wide displacement from metaphor, symbolism, and excitement, posing another problem we confront; it requires the presence of a known lexical language familiar to readers with general experience in the natural physical and medical sciences and the intuitions of time that formed a historical and visionary element in the novel in terms of time and place. The title thus becomes an intriguing element threatening to confuse the reader because suspense plays with the structure. As it does so, it can risk it and glorify it, if we may say so—it's genuine tension for the perceiver, thus representing the system in its fragility, not the chain. It completes the idea of language itself, seeming more emotionally thrilling; it's what seems more thoughtful. As suspense takes intricate twists and turns, it slips evasively from the grasp of the signified because the reader, possessing absolute freedom, links the text to various contexts, creating diverse and conflicting contexts. Each reading becomes a challenge to the reader's memory, following the twists of the sign, slipping away from the grip of the signified, because the reader is one who possesses absolute freedom to link the text to sequences of meaning to the utmost pleasure and delight. This enables them to reproduce the meaning."

In this manner, the novelist seized the reader's mind, manipulating it regardless of the interpretations that might arise about the intriguing action of "A'ishquni" (Love Me), which plays with the reader's thoughts. It's a love, but not a narcissistic one; it's for another entity entirely, a character saved from material existence to appear in emotional and psychological existence, as we later discover in the novel. This love doesn't resemble Nero's narcissism, throwing himself into the river upon seeing his own reflection, as the Greek myth narrates.

The writer succeeded in delicately handling her language and its sensation without disrupting the story's structure, while still preserving scientific terms. Scientific text reflects the mind, whereas literary text expresses emotions, and these challenges held by Sanaa Al-Shaalan were expertly overcome through her linguistic skills and engaging style.

She utilizes language as a tool to generate meaning, exploring its suggestive and connotative potentials to construct the narrative image and solidify the imaginative discourse of the novel. She presents us with a unique mirror to confirm that storytelling is a literature that crafts its language from within the constraints of language itself as an imaginative tool.

Through the transformation of the protagonist into a dual-gendered being loving themselves, we perceive a metaphysical contradiction between the self and the other, only achievable through the presence of another "I." This apparent contradiction leads us into a philosophical discussion about the self and the other, and also serves as a protest against the reality of the murder of the novel's heroine. In reality, the protagonist "I" represents herself as the other to bring forth existence in its entirety.

Gender transformation is not a new theme in

world and Arabic literature; it's present in numerous stories and myths. Transforming from a human into another being occurs in various novels, such as Franz Kafka's "Metamorphosis" or Mikhail Bulgakov's "Heart of a Dog," where a professor undergoes a surgical procedure transferring a spinal gland from a recently killed man to a dog's brain, transforming the dog into a human."

The divergence in the novel 'Love Me' in transforming the protagonist's gender into a pregnant woman wasn't based on fantasy but on a possible scientific imagination. We exist in a different moment in scientific evolution, an unusual moment that could lend credibility to such a transformation, even if in the realm of fiction justified both prospectively and scientifically by the novel. It shouldn't escape us that these novels converge in exposing human oppression and injustice, highlighting human emotions to comprehend the prevailing tyranny. It's a blatant dark fantasy employed by the novelist within the realm of speculative scientific fiction, convincingly used to enlighten the reader on what it narrates, how it narrates, and the storytelling style. As expressed by the Peruvian novelist Mario Vargas Llosa, 'A novel's power of persuasion is greater the more independent and sovereign it appears to its reader, hinting that everything happening within it transpires based on an internal mechanism of narrative imagination, not by external authoritarian force. When a novel feels self-sufficient, containing all it needs to thrive, it has reached the utmost persuasive capacity, successfully seducing its readers into believing what it tells them.'

Yousa links the effectiveness of novelistic creativity to two traits: coherence and a sense of necessity. The narrative in a novel might lack coherence, but the manner in which it's expressed must possess it, allowing the absence of coherence to appear as natural and a part of life. This is what I perceived as a reader of the novel on multiple occasions, alongside everything else it presents.

I'll note two essential observations on my critical approach to literary works or the analysis of texts. It's not necessary for the critic to narrate the events of the novel or the story to the reader to reveal the aesthetic elements and artistic values of the work. The reader shouldn't strain themselves or waste time on critical studies before reading artistic works and evaluated texts, understanding that the language of criticism holds value equal to that of the text itself. Roland Barthes expressed it as "Metalanguage" as the equivalent of "Metanarrative," clarifying this idea.

The critic's role lies in deploying their dynamic abilities in reading texts and examining the contradictory connotations within the boundaries and spaces of the work. Criticism can never follow definitive laws as in science; art and literature create a particular state of consciousness, encompassing knowledge and science within its structure and formation.

The critic's work stems from philosophy; they seek the beauty within the evaluated work, becoming akin to a philosopher with obligations that demand the artist prove whether their work is a good deed or a means to good, where beauty itself is good, and the values of goodness stem from the beauty itself.

This requires an awareness imbued with a range of cognitive factors to attain the pleasure derived from reading, even in 'critiques' that we're keen on reading without interruption after experiencing any literary work or viewing artistic creations or movies.

Therefore, the critic's task isn't preachy or proselytizing; it's an exploration of the core of the text, which constitutes the basis of aesthetic experience and its source. As Clive Bell said: 'When we try to comprehend an artwork aesthetically, we mustn't taste or judge the artwork from the standpoint of our personal interests, beliefs, emotions, or cultural biases, but from the perspective of the artwork itself and based on the inherent qualities or attributes present in its significant form. In other words, we must objectively taste the artwork itself for the sake of itself. This is the aesthetic integrity through which we achieve the highest levels of pleasure in reading and aesthetic emotions. The novel 'Love Me' is an added experience to the genre of scientific fiction in the Arab world, which suffers from scarcity. There haven't been many books with this kind of narrative storytelling and fiction, scarcely more than one can count on their fingers.

Amidst the scientific advancements and technological progress witnessed by humanity, we are in dire need of this kind of novel, considering that every text has its backbone and uniqueness, constituting a new added experience, and must originate from within the cultural and social context of the human experiment."

Exploring Literary Depth: Unveiling the Narrative Complexities in "Love Me"

Literature, as a mirror to societal evolution and human consciousness, continually stretches its boundaries, defying conventional norms, and intriguingly engaging readers through multifaceted narratives. "Love Me," a captivating novel, transcends the realms of traditional storytelling by delving into uncharted territories of speculative imagination, scientific plausibility, and socio-philosophical introspection.

The novel's deviation from norms emerges not merely from the realm of fantasy but from a credible scientific imagination. Its narrative choice, transforming the protagonist's gender into that of a pregnant woman, isn't an esoteric dive into fantastical realms but rather a plausible outcome in an era of unparalleled scientific advancement. This divergence from conventionality is justified prospectively and scientifically within the fabric of the novel.

Within its intricate storytelling, "Love Me" shares a common thread with several narratives by laying bare the human oppression and injustices, while also spotlighting the spectrum of human emotions to elucidate the prevailing tyranny. It ventures into the realm of dark fantasy, compellingly articulated within the framework of speculative scientific fiction. The novelist astutely uses this narrative tool to enlighten readers about the storyline, its execution, and the art of storytelling itself.

Echoing the sentiments of Mario Vargas Llosa,

the persuasiveness of a novel lies in its apparent independence and sovereignty to the reader. When events within it seem to unfold organically through an internal mechanism of narrative imagination, it achieves its utmost persuasive potential, effortlessly seducing readers into the belief of its narrative.

Critical discourse on literary works often embarks on elucidating aesthetic elements and artistic values rather than a mere recounting of events. Roland Barthes' concept of "Metalanguage" aligns with this notion, emphasizing the intrinsic value of criticism akin to the language of the text itself.

The role of the critic is akin to that of a philosopher, delving into the core of the text to unravel its inherent beauty and artistic merits. This pursuit demands a heightened cognitive awareness to derive pleasure from the act of reading, engaging with the text objectively and appreciating its aesthetic nuances.

Criticism, therefore, becomes an exploration within the boundaries and spaces of the text, devoid of definitive laws akin to scientific disciplines. Art and literature create a unique state of consciousness where knowledge and science amalgamate within its structure and formation.

Moreover, the critic's responsibility transcends mere judgment; it's a quest to unveil the intrinsic qualities of the text, experiencing its aesthetic integrity, and deriving pleasure independent of personal biases or cultural inclinations.

In essence, "Love Me" serves as an enigmatic

addition to the realm of scientific fiction in the Arab world, offering a narrative that defies scarcity in its genre. Its narrative complexities and philosophical introspection challenge readers to explore the intricacies of speculative imagination, social relevance, and the evolving human experience.

As literature adapts and evolves, narratives like "Love Me" stand as a testament to its ever-expanding horizons. They underscore the significance of narratives rooted in cultural and social contexts while embracing the dynamic interplay between speculative imagination, scientific plausibility, and human introspection. Such narratives not only entertain but also provoke critical contemplation, enriching our understanding of the world and the human condition.

Bibliography

Al-Attas, S. M. N. (1993). Islam and secularism. Kuala Lumpur: ISTAC.

Al-Dimasyqi, A.-I. A.-N. (2016). Syarh Shahih Muslim. Dar al-Kutub al-`Ilmiyah.

Allen, C. (2013). Islamophobia. In Islamophobia. https://doi.org/10.4324/9781315745077-41

al-Maraghi, M. (2002). Tafsir al-Maraghi. Beirut: Darul Fikir.

Al-Qaradawi, Y. (2010). Islam an introduction. Kuala Lumpur: Islamic Book Trust.

al-Qurtubi, A. A. M. ibn A. (2014). Tafsir al-Qurtubi (Vol. 20). Beirut: Dar al-Kutub al-'Ilmiyah.

Al-Qushayri, I. (2018). Tafsir al-Qushayri. Dar Ihya' al -Turath al-Arabi.

Al-Rāzī, F. (2000). Al-Tafsīr al-Kabīr aw Mafātih al-Gayb, Vol. VII. Dar Al-Hadith.

Al-Sya'rawi, A.-I. A.-M. (2007). Tafsir Al-Sya'rawi. Qitha' al-Saqafah wa al-Kutub.

Al-Syawkani, M. bin A. (2014). Fath al-Qadir al-Jami' baina Fannai al-Riwayah wa al-Dirayah min 'Ilm al-Tafsir, Vol. 5. Dar Ibnu Hazim.

Al-Thabathaba'i. (1987). Tafsir Al-Mizan. Islamic Publications Office.

Al-Zuhaily, W. (2009). Al-Tafsir al-Munir fi al-Aqidah wa al-Syariah wa al-Manhaj. Dar al-Fikr.

APS (Applied Social Psychology). (2017). The Role of Religion in Prejudice Enablement and Reduction. Retrieved December 26, 2022, from https://sites.psu.edu/aspsy/2017/09/28/the-role-of-religion-in-prejudice-enablement-and-reduction/

Bakhshi Hazrat 'Alī Aḥmed and Rizwānur Raḥmān. (2012). Glimpses of the Holy Qur'ān. (New Delhi: Adam Publishers and Distributors).

Chelini-Pont, B. (2013). Relationship between Stereotyping and the Place of Religion in the Public Sphere. In J. Svartvik, Jesper & Wiren (Ed.), Religious Stereotyping and Interreligious Relations (pp. 75–84). Palgrave Macmillan.

Geertz, C. (1977). The Interpretation of Cultures. Basic Books.

Geertz, C. (2013). Religion as a cultural system. In Anthropological Approaches to the Study of Religion (pp. 1–46). https://doi.org/10.4324/9781315017570

Hanafi, H. (2000). Islam in the modern world: Religion, ideology and development vol. I. Cairo: Dar Kabaa.

Hanafi, H. (2006). Culture and civilizations, conflict or dialogue? Vol. I the meridian thought. Cairo: Book Center for Publishing.

Jafari, F. (2020). Theological knowledge in Islamic mysticism and gnosticism." Kanz Philosophia A Journal for Islamic Philosophy and Mysticism 6(2). DOI: https://doi.org/10.20871/kpjipm.v6i2.92.

Karama, M. J., & Khater, N. A. (2020). Educational peace theory in the holy qur'an. Al-Bayān – Journal of Qurʾān and Ḥadīth Studies, 18, 138–154. http://scholar.ppu.edu/bitstream/handle/12345678

9/2214/1.pdf?sequence=1&isAllowed=y

Khairulnizam, M., & Saili, S. (2009). Inter-faith dialogue: The qur'anic and prophetic perspective. Journal of Usuluddin, 9(2), 65–94.

Khaldun, I. (2015). Muqaddimah. Cairo: Dar-Ibnu al-Aitam.

Kidwai, Salim. (1996). Hindustani Mufassirein Awr Unki' Arabi Tafsirein (in Urdu) .(New Delhi:Maktaba Jamiah).

Kokan, Moḥammad Yousuf. (1960). Arabic and Persian in Carnatic, (Madras: Hafiza House).

Ma'roof M M M. (1995). *Spoken Tamil dialect of the Muslims of Sri Lanka: Language as Identity classifier*. Islamic Studies 34 (4).

Nashir, H. (2015). Understanding the ideology of Muhammadiyah. Muhammadiyah University Press.

Nieuwkerk, K. van, LeVine, M., & Stokes, M. (2016). Islam and popular culture. University of Texas Press.

Patji, A. R. (1991). The Arabs of Surabaya: a study of sociocultural integration. Canberra: Australian

National University.

Putra, A. D., Purnomo, D., & Utomo, A. W. (2019). Sociological study of harmony in diversity: Lessons from Salatiga. Walisongo: Jurnal Penelitian Sosial Keagamaan, 27(1), 69–98. 10.21580/ws.27.1.3504

Ridwan, M., & Robikah, S. (2019). Ethical vision of the qur'an: Interpreting concept of the qur'anic sociology in developing religious harmony. Jurnal Ilmiah Islam Futura, 18(2), 308–326. http://dx.doi.org/10.22373/jiif.v19i2.5444

Sanaa Sha'lan, 'Adore Me'(A'shaquni), Daira al-Maktaba al- Wataniyya, Hashemite Kingdom of Jordan, Third Edition, 2016.

Saerozi, M. (2017). Dynamics of the development of istiqomah mosque in front of a church in Ungaran Central Java Indonesia. Journal of Indonesian Islam, 11(02), 423–458. 10.15642/JIIS.2017.11.2.423-458

Saged, A. A. (2021). Honoring the human self with a world peace study in the light of purposes the holy quran. Quranika: Journal of Libahuts Qur'an, 19(2), 223–234.

Shareef, Moḥammed Muṣṭafa and Bad'iuddin Ṣabri. (2008). Development of Tafseer Literature in India, (Hyderabad: Osmania University).

Shihab, M. Q. (2004). Tafsir al-mishbah. Jakarta: Lentera Hati.

Shu'aib, Tayka. (1993). Arabic, Arwi and Persian in Sarandib and Tamil Nadu, (Chennai: Imaamul Aroos Trust).
Thabari, I. J. (1999). Tafsir al Thabari. Kairo: Dar al Fikr.

Zamakhsyari, M. I. U. al. (2012). Al-kassyaf 'an haqaiq al-tanzil wa 'uyun al-ta'wil fi wujuh al-ta'wil. Cairo: Dar al-Hadis.

Zubair, K M A Aḥamed. (2010). *Tamil-Arabic Relationship*, ed. John Samuel G, (Chennai:The Institute of Asian Studies Press).
Zubair, K M A Ahamed. (2012). *Eminent Scholars of Sheik Sadaqathullah Appa's Family and their*

contribution to Arabic and Islamic Studies, (in Arabic), Thaqafatul ḥind 54, (3&4).

Zubair, K M A Ahamed. (2013). *Qasaid al-Madaih al-Nabaviyya fi Tamil Nadu,* (in Arabic), Thaqafatul ḥind 64, (4).

Zubair, K M A Aḥamed. (2017). Prophet's Panegyrics in Arabic Literature, (Moldova: Lambert Academic Publishing).

Printed by Books on Demand GmbH, Norderstedt / Germany